CONTEMPORARY STANDARDS

10 REFRESHING SETTINGS

ARRANGED BY MARIANNE KIM

ISBN 978-1-5400-5797-6

Visit Hal Leonard Online at
www.halleonard.com

Contact us:
Hal Leonard
7777 West Bluemound Road
Milwaukee, WI 53213
Email: info@halleonard.com

In Europe, contact:
Hal Leonard Europe Limited
42 Wigmore Street
Marylebone, London, W1U 2RN
Email: info@halleonardeurope.com

In Australia, contact:
Hal Leonard Australia Pty. Ltd.
4 Lentara Court
Cheltenham, Victoria, 3192 Australia
Email: info@halleonard.com.au

BLESS THE BROKEN ROAD

Words and Music by MARCUS HUMMON,
BOBBY BOYD and JEFF HANNA
Arranged by Marianne Kim

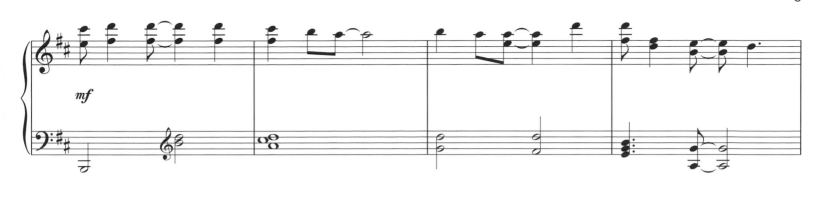

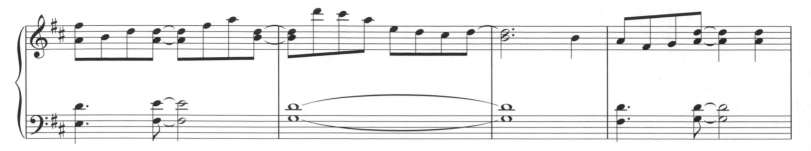

DON'T KNOW WHY

Words and Music by
JESSE HARRIS
Arranged by Marianne Kim

HALLELUJAH

Words and Music by
LEONARD COHEN
Arranged by Marianne Kim

JUST THE WAY YOU ARE

Words and Music by
BILLY JOEL
Arranged by Marianne Kim

Moderately (♩ = 126)

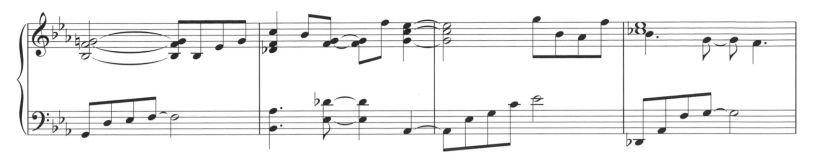

MY HEART WILL GO ON
(Love Theme from 'Titanic')

Music by JAMES HORNER
Lyric by WILL JENNINGS
Arranged by Marianne Kim

Gently (♩ = 100)

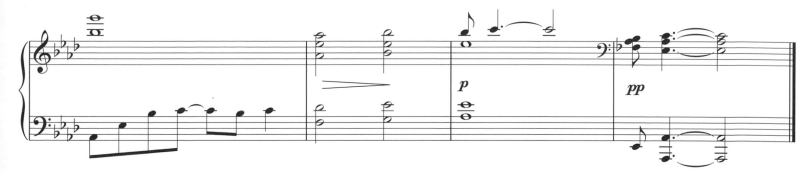

THE SOUND OF SILENCE

Words and Music by
PAUL SIMON
Arranged by Marianne Kim

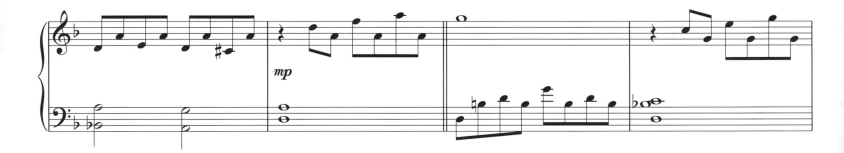

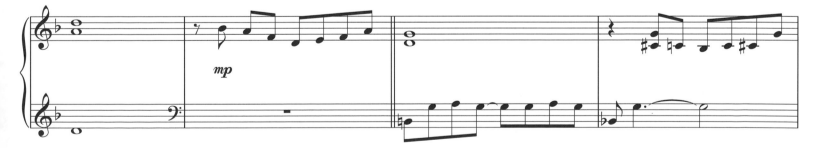

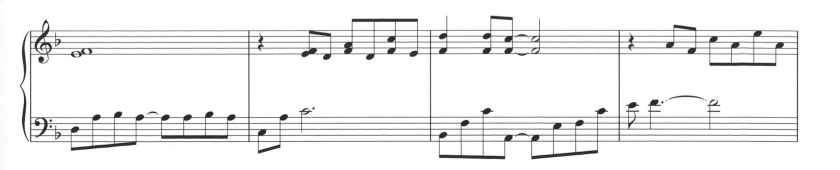

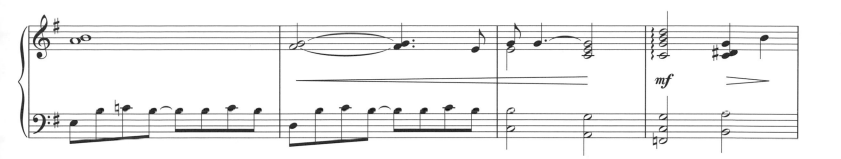

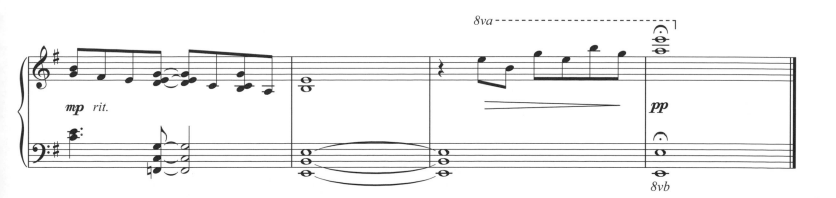

THINKING OUT LOUD

Words and Music by ED SHEERAN
and AMY WADGE
Arranged by Marianne Kim

Steady Pop feel (♩ = 78)

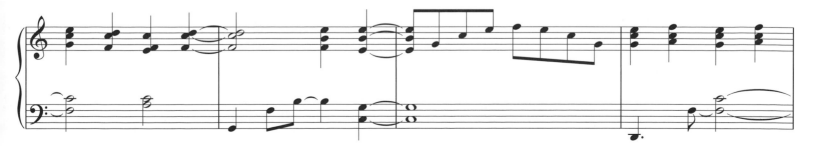

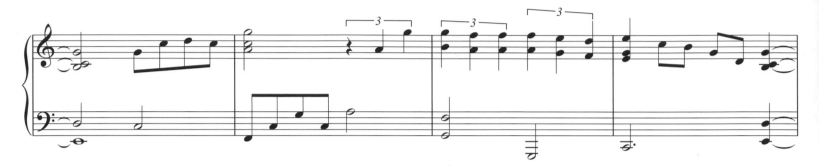

WHAT A WONDERFUL WORLD

Words and Music by GEORGE DAVID WEISS
and BOB THIELE
Arranged by Marianne Kim

Moderately (♩. = 60)

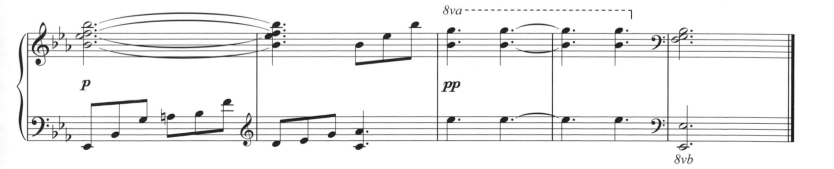

YOU RAISE ME UP

Words and Music by BRENDAN GRAHAM
and ROLF LOVLAND
Arranged by Marianne Kim

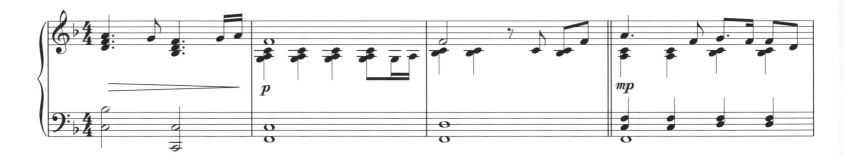

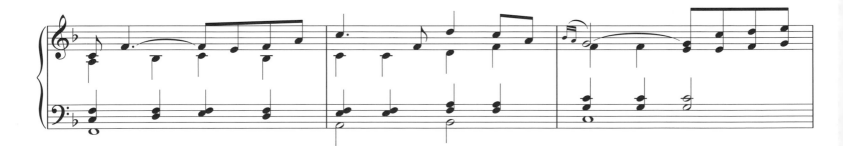

YESTERDAY

Words and Music by JOHN LENNON
and PAUL McCARTNEY
Arranged by Marianne Kim

Gently (♩ = 92)

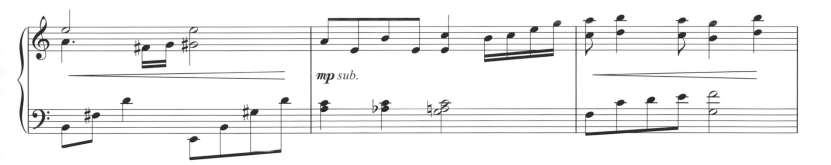